World's
TRICKIEST
PUZZLES

Charles Barry Townsend

Sterling Publishing Co., Inc. New York

This book is dedicated to our family's California connection, Jane and George Cleveland.

Library of Congress Cataloging-in-Publication Data

Townsend, Charles Barry.
   World's trickiest puzzles / by Charles Barry Townsend.
      p.   cm.
   Includes index.
   ISBN 0-8069-0964-1
   1. Puzzles—Juvenile literature. I. Title.
GV1493.T69   1995
793.73—dc20
                         95-17934
                            CIP
                            AC

10 9 8 7 6 5 4 3 2 1

Published by Sterling Publishing Company, Inc.
387 Park Avenue South, New York, N.Y. 10016
©1995 by Charles Barry Townsend
Distributed in Canada by Sterling Publishing
% Canadian Manda Group, One Atlantic Avenue, Suite 105
Toronto, Ontario, Canada M6K 3E7
Distributed in Great Britain and Europe by Cassell PLC
Wellington House, 125 Strand, London WC2R 0BB, England
Distributed in Australia by Capricorn Link (Australia) Pty Ltd.
P.O. Box 6651, Baulkham Hills, Business Centre, NSW 2153, Australia
Manufactured in the United States of America
All rights reserved

Sterling ISBN 0-8069-0964-1

Contents

Introduction

Greetings, fellow puzzle enthusiasts. This book is something of a milestone for me, being the tenth volume in my series of puzzle books for Sterling. When I set out to write these books I intended to present my readers with a collection of the finest puzzles and problems that have challenged thinking people for the past 100 years. This volume adds another 96 brain-busters to the list. Not all these puzzles are venerable problems of the past. I've created several new items, as well. You'll also find over a hundred detailed and amusing illustrations to liven up the presentation.

In this book you'll travel back in time to our favorite diner to match wits with Hash House Harriet, check out the spying methods of J. Pinkerton Snoopington, play a game of checkers with Mr. Fogg, learn how Joan Crawford would handle a job application, and attend the "Riddle Ball" at the famous old Palm House. Then it's off for a Mediterranean cruise, a stop in the Old West for a Flaming Comet cocktail, and then a chance to win a wager against that Prince of Con Men, J. Wellington Moneybags. Other problems deal with phrenology, archaeology, the Second World War, chess, the circus, farming, and the machinations of a Mad Scientist. All in all, you're in for an exciting adventure in Puzzleland.

Find a nice comfortable chair, a supply of pencils and paper, and hang a "Do Not Disturb" sign on your door for the next few hours. It's time to do battle with *The World's Trickiest Puzzles!*

PUZZLES

World's Trickiest "Checkers" Puzzle

Mr. Fogg is a hard man to beat. At their last game the senator thought he had a sure win but Fogg made short work of him. It was Fogg's move and he was playing the black checkers. White was moving up the board while black was moving down. What were Fogg's winning moves?

World's Trickiest "Joan Crawford" Puzzle

"Just listen to this question on your job application form: 'What is the only word in the dictionary that begins with SEX and has nothing to do with either sex or six?' What jerk thought up this quiz? I'm a woman of the 30s who's shouldered her way past hundreds of men in dozens of pictures. No two-bit psychological test is going to stop me this time either. And furthermore, what's the answer to that dumb question anyway?"

"But, Ms. Crawford, but, Ms. Crawford, but, but, but . . . !"

World's Trickiest "Stereoscope" Puzzle

World's Trickiest "Stereoscope" Puzzle

Calven Collectable, while checking out a new batch of stereoscope views, noticed that the picture on the right side of the card wasn't the same as the one on the left. Eleven items were missing. Can you find them?

World's Trickiest "Ladder" Puzzles

"In 'Ladder Puzzles' you're required to change the top word into the bottom word by changing one letter at a time as you go down the ladder. Each change must produce a new word."

"These are great boards you made up, Mike! We can use them at next week's Puzzle Fair! Linda, how many 'Ladder Puzzles' have we made up so far?"

"So far, Biff, we have five puzzles. They are: in four moves change SICK to WELL; in five moves change BIRD to NEST and PIG to STY; and, finally, in six moves change MINE to COAL and CITY to FARM. Do you have any more to add, Mike?"

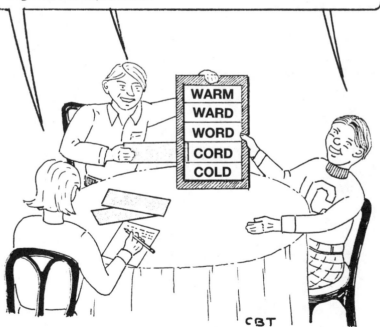

World's Trickiest "Dragon" Puzzle

"So I had these three knights trapped inside Old Misery Cave. I had them pinned up against the wall with my tail and I said, 'I'm Cedric, the guardian dragon of St. Basil's treasure. Answer the following three questions correctly and the gold is yours. Fail, and you'll never leave this cave alive.

   1. What song do you get when you cross the Ape Man with a zebra?
   2. How do you make a hippopotamus float?
   3. In the following series of numbers what number comes next: 1, 4, 3 . . . ?'

"Now, you in the poorly fitting suit of armor, what's your answer to the first question?"

"Gosh, Grandpa, what happened next? Did you roast them? Did you toast them?"

World's Trickiest "Tea Chest" Puzzle

This old chestnut is called "The Enchanted Tea Chest Puzzle." The small paper box pictured here is constructed of six rectangular pieces of light cardboard. Playing cards are perfect for it. The two narrow ends of each card are folded up at a ninety-degree angle. The rest of each card should form a perfect square. Once you've "locked" the six cards together you'll find that the box is quite secure and can be thrown around without having it fall apart. No glue is used in the construction. It's easy to put together when you know how, but the novice will have his hands full trying to solve it. If you need help you'll find it in the Answers section.

World's Trickiest "Restaurant" Puzzle

> *"I've had it! First the Benson twins, as usual, skipped out on paying their share of the bill, and now I'm treated to a chicken gumbo shower. This club has seen the last of Frederick Highcollar."*

Every Monday the Good Samaritan Club would meet for lunch. Before the check arrived the Benson twins would always be called away on business. On the day that Freddy took his bath, the remaining diners were presented with a bill for $80.00. It was their custom to divide the bill up equally among those present. To cover the Benson twins' share, each member had to pay an additional $2.00. How many people originally sat down to lunch?

World's Trickiest "Quotation" Puzzle

O	I	N	T	U	S	O	E

O
F
N
I
S
B
A
S
N
A
D

Y
U
L
Q
L
O
E
N
T
E

D	S	I	K	L	M	L	E

It's been reported that when the famous German spy of World War I, Mata Hari, was being questioned about her activities she coyly answered with the famous quotation hidden in the frame of letters that surrounds this page. To find it, start at any letter and go around the frame twice, reading every other letter.

World's Trickiest "Kite" Puzzle

It's relaxation time down at the Puzzle Club and Mr. Okito, the resident expert on Japanese puzzles, is showing off his latest creation. Can you beat the other "experts" to the solution? How many different-size equilateral triangles are in the kite's construction?

World's Trickiest "Hidden Word" Puzzles

Hidden in the comments at the bottom of each picture is the locality of the incident depicted. You have one minute to find the name of each place.

World's Trickiest "Sledding" Puzzle

Harry and Harriet barely missed meeting up with the Brody Bunch while participating in the West Orange Downhill Sled Races. Over a measured one-mile course Harry's new sled made the run two and a half times faster than the Brodys' older bobsled. Harry and Harriet beat them out by six minutes. Given these scant facts, can the reader figure out how long it took each contestant to run the one-mile course?

World's Trickiest "Bow Tie" Puzzle

For years "Bow Tie" Barlow made—and won—hundreds of bets on the speed with which he could tie a perfect bow tie. However, last night he met his match when J. Wellington Moneybags drew the above picture of a bow tie and bet Barlow he couldn't duplicate the drawing using one continuous line that didn't cross itself at any point or go back over any part already drawn. Could you have succeeded where Barlow proved to be all thumbs?

World's Trickiest "Stick" Puzzle

Over the years the above problem seems to have been a sure attention getter. All you need are 36 ice cream sticks and a lot of patience. Lay out the sticks, as shown above, so that they form thirteen squares. Now, remove eight sticks so you're left with just six squares.

World's Trickiest "Famous Sayings" Puzzle

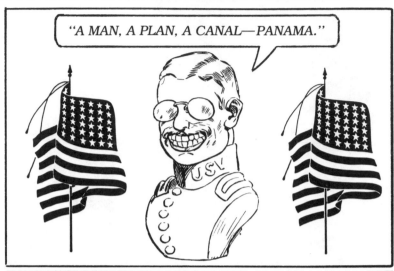

What do these two famous sayings by prominent leaders of history have in common?

World's Trickiest "Riddle" Puzzles

"What was the greatest feat of strength?"

"Who is bigger, Mr. Bigger, or his baby?"

"When is a boat like a heap of snow?"

"Why is an old one-dollar watch like a river?"

During the "Riddle Ball," at the Palm House in 1896, whenever the music stopped you asked your partner a riddle.

World's Trickiest "Diner" Puzzle

Well, here we are at our favorite diner in Bloomfield, New Jersey. And there's Hash House Harriet calling out a customer's order using the colorful diner lingo of years gone by. We've arranged the sentence to form an interesting puzzle for you to solve. Replace each letter with a number, using the same number each time the same letter appears, to make a correct mathematical expression. Also, see if you can figure out what the order is for.

World's Trickiest "Golf Tees" Puzzle

> *"Ever since Andrew MacDivot made that golf tee bet with me last week I can't concentrate on my game. At this rate, I'll never win another club tournament!"*

Nelda Niblick, the lofty amateur women's champion of the Idle Hours Country Club, has been put off her game by one of Andrew MacDivot's famous 19th-hole wagers. He bet Nelda a new set of irons that she couldn't arrange 24 golf tees in such a manner that they would form four perfect squares. Can you help her beat MacDivot at his own game before tee-off time?

World's Trickiest "Word Square" Puzzle

"Beware, problem solvers! It is I, the Masked Puzzler, and I'm back to challenge you with one of the world's oldest word puzzles. Pictured on my mask is a six-letter word square. The same six words appear both horizontally and vertically. To cloud your minds so you can't see the answer, I've scrambled the letters in each of the words. However, I'm not without a modicum of mercy. Below are helpful hints regarding the meaning of each word."

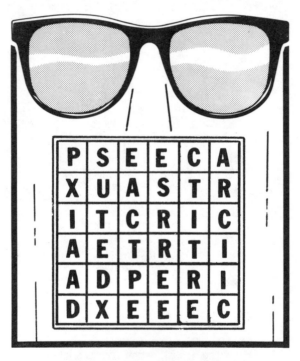

1. What a famous magician did.
2. An extra load to bear.
3. He who sits in judgment.
4. The best clothing.
5. Having something in common.
6. To outdo all others. (Old spelling)

World's Trickiest "Matchstick" Puzzle

Here is the arrival of the American Puzzle Club at the 1879 International Exhibition in Sydney, Australia. The matchstick puzzle on the side of the balloon won first prize. The problem is to arrange 14 matches so they form five diamond-shaped figures all the same size. The matches cannot be broken or overlapped in any way.

World's Trickiest "Puzzle Spy" Puzzle

Also at the exhibition was the infamous J. Pinkerton Snoopington, seller of puzzle secrets. With his patented invention, the Snooper Phone, he could eavesdrop on puzzle officials as they were making up contest questions. Let's listen in, too. ". . .Then we're all agreed: Question number 25 is, 'What word is formed if we add the same three letters to the front and the back of the letters ---ERGRO---? The word thus formed is familiar to everyone living in London."

Let the record show that Snoopington was thrown out of the country before he could peddle his info. Do you know the answer to this purloined question?

World's Trickiest "Word" Puzzle

"An excellent meal, my good crustacean! However, I seem to have left my wallet down below. How about a small wager, say double-or-nothing, for the price of the bill?"

"You're always short of clams, Mr. Bass. Twice this week you've hooked me like this. Very well, what's the wager?"

"I'll bet you can't tell me what the words fedora, upon, sprouts, and jihad have in common before Mildred and I finish this fine bottle of kelp wine!"

Can the reader net the answer before closing time?

World's Trickiest "Cloth" Puzzle

"Try to stay awake, Barton. Old Feziwig will fire you if he sees you dozing on the job!"

"I can't help it. I was up all night trying to solve the cloth puzzle our draper challenged me with yesterday!"

Barton Bolt is having his problems. The store's draper bet him he couldn't take a square piece of cloth of any size and cut it into several pieces that could then be used to form three smaller squares of material. The draper said Barton could make only two straight cuts across the cloth. Finally, one of these squares was to be formed by sewing two of the pieces together along one edge of the material.

Can you weave a solution to Barton's problem?

World's Trickiest "Beheading" Puzzle

Professor Albert is explaining how his new "Word Beheading" opera is to be sung. The work is derived from the old "Beheading" game where the puzzler is told to chop off the first letter of a word in order to form another. Here are the subjects of the eight arias to be sung:

1. Behead to ascend and leave ascend.
2. Behead shut to make mislay.
3. Behead rebuke to make chilly.
4. Behead a server to make a beam.
5. Behead a vessel to make part of a fence.
6. Behead a vehicle to get an animal.
7. Behead a noisemaker and get a drink.
8. Behead a vessel and get a belt holder.

World's Trickiest "Betting" Puzzle

> "That was a fine meal, Arbuthnot. Well worth the $111.00 the bill comes to. Why don't we have a wager to determine who gets to pay for it? I'll bet you the cost of our two dinners that you can't calculate in your head in 15 seconds what two-thirds of three-fourths of the bill comes to!"

> "You're on, Wendell. Start timing me now!"

The reader is also on the clock.

World's Trickiest "Telephone" Puzzle

"Hi, Tim! I just met the new family that moved in next door. You wanted to know how many kids there were so I've made up a puzzle you can work on while I'm coming over to your house. Each of the boys has as many sisters as he has brothers, while each of the girls has twice as many brothers as she has sisters. I'll bet you ten marbles you can't solve it before I get to your house!"

Back when the telephone was young, a boy could have his own private line for only a dollar. That would get him two Perfection Transmitters, three hundred feet of wire and a dozen loops to hold the wire on the posts. Try to match that bargain today.

World's Trickiest "Ports of Call" Puzzle

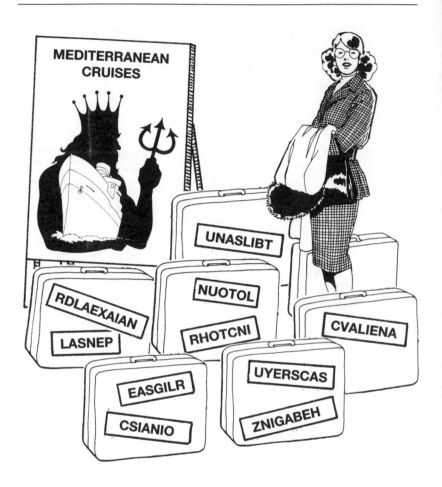

Gwendolyn Globetrotter is back from her three-week tour of the Mediterranean. Her tour docked at 10 of the most famous cities in the region. We've made a puzzle of her travels by scrambling the letters in the city names that appear on her luggage stickers. Let's see if you can unscramble them before Gwendolyn can find a cab out of the airport.

World's Trickiest "Bar Room" Puzzle

FLAMING COMET
$1.15

Many a strange concoction was served up in the Gold Rush saloons of the Old West. Here we see a mixologist dispensing a flaming libation called a "Flaming Comet." After one you're seeing stars. Newcomers were given a chance to get one free if they could come up with the $1.15 using only six coins. The hitch was that with these coins you *couldn't* make change for a dollar, a half dollar, a quarter, a dime or a nickel. You have until the flames die down to solve this one, pardner!

World's Trickiest "Money" Puzzle

Mayor Brogan was a man of great honesty. The other day he went into his favorite haberdashery store and said to the man in the hat department, "I want that $10.00 hat in the window. If you lend me as much money as I have in my pocket I'll buy it."

The salesman said OK and gave him the money. The mayor then paid cash for the hat. Next he went to the suit department and bought a $10.00 jacket using the same proposition. On the way out he stopped in the shoe department and bought a $10.00 pair of shoes, paying in the same way. When he left the store he had no money in his pockets.

How much money did Brogan have when he first entered the store?

World's Trickiest "Rebus" Puzzle

"Well, Farquhar, here is the jumping-off place for our special agents. The last coded message we received was: 'Captain BBBB arrived in the DWDEDSDTD today with his CCCC.' Have you heard anything more about their whereabouts?"

"Well, Liverston, the agent apparently never made contact with the enemy. My agent down there smuggled out the following message last night: 'Captain BBBB mission a bust. NAR EH HE RAN across the island, like EDalienEN, finding 023456789.' "

Can you decipher the above coded messages being discussed by these two turn-of-the-century secret service agents?

World's Trickiest "Nails" Puzzle

During the renovation of the old Abelard mansion the local handyman, Hiram Ballpeene, won a peck of bets with his nail puzzles. Take the one above, for instance. Hiram laid out 16 finishing nails in the form of five squares and bet the masonry foreman lunch for a week that he couldn't move one of the nails to a new position so six squares would be formed. Try to plumb the answer before quitting time.

World's Trickiest "Weighing" Puzzle

"This is really a neat puzzle that your father, Professor Kane, challenged us to solve. We have to find out which one of these nine lead weights was incorrectly made. Eight of them each weighs exactly 16 ounces, while the ninth one weighs only 15¾ ounces!"

"That's right, Mike, and we're only allowed to use this scale when looking for the short weight. The problem would be easy if we could weigh two of them at a time until we found the light one, but Dad said we had to do it in just two weighings. I think now's the time for one of your patented hunches!"

World's Trickiest "Fishing" Puzzle

Four of the guests at Ma Boscomb's boarding house—Calvin, Wylie, Emmet, and Quentin—went fishing down at Moran's Creek. Altogether they caught 10 fish. When they gave their catch to Ma to put in her freezer she noticed that:

1. Calvin had caught more than Quentin.
2. Wylie and Emmet gave her as many fish as Calvin and Quentin.
3. Calvin and Wylie had caught fewer fish than Emmet and Quentin.

Given these facts can you figure out how many fish each of the boarders caught that day?

World's Trickiest "Poor Sport" Puzzle

"I beat you again, Lionel, and I'll always beat you, whether it's in cards, chess, or any other of life's endeavors that may find us pitted against one another!"

"Confound it, Jeffreys, they ought to invent an ____iperspir____ to combat your offensive personality. The only thing that you really excel in is being the world's greatest ____men____!"

In the above acerbic exchange Jeffreys finally got the better of Lionel by challenging him to play an old word game. The two partially completed words in his rejoinder are missing the same three letters at the beginning and end. The letters are also in the same order. Each word has a different set of letters to find.

World's Trickiest "Sport" Puzzle

Norma Nettlesworth was the acknowledged queen of women's amateur sports during the 1902 social season in Newport. She won or captained the winning team in no less than 20 events. She was particularly good at sports that employed a hard, solid ball.

Years later, while being interviewed about that season, she said, "I recall 12 events that were played with a solid ball that year. If you can name at least nine of them I'll consider you well versed in competitive sports."

I believe the reporter failed her test. Would the reader care to take up the challenge?

World's Trickiest "What" Puzzles

When the Watts gave one of their famous riddle dinner parties you were expected to come with at least a half dozen "What" questions to help enliven the festivities.

World's Trickiest "Toy Train" Puzzle

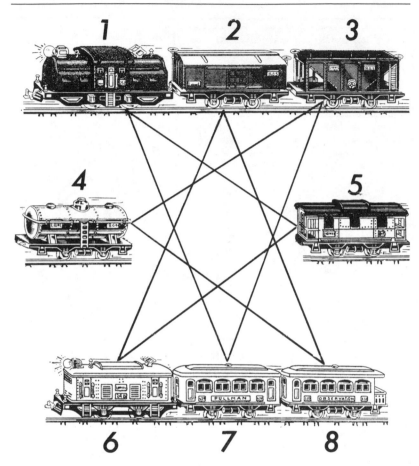

Pictured here are eight old Lionel toy train locomotives and cars. We've linked them together with six lengths of track so we can present the reader with an interesting problem in car switching. First, place two dimes on cars 1 and 3, and then place two pennies on cars 6 and 8. Moving one coin at a time along the tracks, make the coins change places. At no time can any two of these coins be on the same car at the same time. You have to solve this puzzle using no more than 16 moves.

World's Trickiest "Legacy" Puzzle

"Gee, Your Honor, how did you solve their problem?"

Judge Fineum had been called in to solve a tricky estate problem. It seems that a wealthy gentleman, on the verge of death, was told by his wife that his two ne'er-do-well sons, Reggie and Farnsworth, were rushing home to be with him at the end. On hearing this the old man had the following will drawn up: If the first to arrive was Reggie, he should receive two-thirds of the estate and the mother one-third. However, if Farnsworth arrived first then he would receive one-third and the mother two-thirds. As it turned out, the old man died within minutes of signing the will and the next day both sons arrived together at the doorstep. How was the estate to be divided, taking into account the wishes of the father, as stated in his will? It was decided that only Judge Fineum could solve this dilemma. What was his solution?

World's Trickiest "Doodle Art" Puzzles

When the crops have been harvested and things get slow around the farm, Cy Corncrib likes to go to town and catch up with any cultural events that may be happening. One day they were have a showing of Doodle Art down at the library. The two pictures that Cy is shown here studying are among the oldest examples of this type of puzzling. What do you think these pictures represent?

World's Trickiest "Quilting" Puzzle

This is another delightful problem by that great turn-of-the-century puzzler, Sam Loyd.

"The children have worked all of their names into a wonderful patch quilt, which they are going to present to their teacher. Commence wherever you please and go from square to square, and see how many names you can discover. You can move vertically, horizontally, or diagonally around the quilt. However, each letter can only be used once in any one name. In our picture if you start at the letter *N*, and follow the line, you will spell out the name NANCY. See if you can find all of the other kids' names in her class."

World's Trickiest "Note" Puzzle

FRIENDS   SIR,   FRIENDS,
STAND YOUR DISPOSITION;
I BEARING
A MAN   THE WORLD
  IS
CONTEMPT,   WHILST THE
          RIDICULE.
          ARE
          AMBITIOUS

YOUR OBEDIENT SERVANT,
ALGERNON BETSALOT.

The above cryptic note, penned to his bookmaker, was Algernon's way of crowing after paying up his racing debts. Can you decode this ancient rebus within the time it took for Algernon to pick the losing nag in the next race?

World's Trickiest "Maze" Puzzle

This puzzle, while not being very hard to solve, is certainly a curiosity. We found it in an 1857 copy of *The Magician's Own Book*. After entering the maze try to reach "Rosamond's Bower" in less than 60 seconds.

World's Trickiest "Candle" Puzzle

"I wish Mr. Wainscoat, our sexton, wouldn't tempt me with these puzzles on Saturday night. I'll never finish my sermon for tomorrow if this one proves to be difficult. And how in the world was he able to fuse these candles together, anyway?"

Reverend I.N. Spire is faced with a dilemma. The sexton wagered him lunch that after laying out 12 candles in the shape of a church and tower he couldn't then shift five of the candles to new positions that would leave him with three squares of equal size. I have a feeling the parishioners are in for a short sermon on Sunday.

World's Trickiest "Triangle" Puzzle

"Once a year my Nana makes me take her old rugs outside and give them a good beating. She calls this one her 'Puzzle Rug' because of the triangular design in it. Think you can solve it in 60 seconds, Mike?"

The problem is to find out how many triangles, great and small, are contained within the pattern. The smaller triangles overlap the larger ones.

World's Trickiest "Square" Puzzle

"Well, Monsieur Count de Numburrs, how did you do with the previous 'Triangle' puzzle? I bet it took you 60 minutes, instead of 60 seconds, to solve it. Here's another problem to test your skills with: 'How many squares will you find on an ordinary chessboard? You can have up to 60 days to figure it out.' "

"As usual, my dear Count de Pomade, your wit is as light as an English plum pudding. Even Fifi here knows that there are 64 squares on a chessboard. No, wait a minute. There are 65, or is it 70, or maybe 75? Anyhow, your question is stupid and I refuse to answer it!"

The reader has six minutes to find the answer.

World's Trickiest "Vowel" Puzzle

During the test, Freddy was given a sheet of paper that had been divided into 25 squares. The squares contained the vowels A, E, I, O, and U repeated five times. The applicant had to cut this sheet into five pieces, each of which would contain a set of these five vowels.

Care to try your luck at getting the position that Freddy missed?

World's Trickiest "Wager" Puzzle

J. Wellington Moneybags dropped into the Jolly Ribman Steak House the other night and caged a meal on the house when he beat out the proprietor, Biff Wellington, with the following nifty wager. After folding a sheet of paper in half twice along the dotted lines indicated above, he handed it to Biff and said; "I've folded this sheet of paper over two times, which gives us four thicknesses of paper. I'll bet you even money you can't tell me beforehand how many pieces of paper you will end up with if you cut this packet in half. Will there be 2, 3, 4, 5 or 6 pieces? You must cut the packet down the center on a line parallel to either of the folded edges. Now, do we have a bet, or are you too chicken to take me on?"

World's Trickiest "Motoring" Puzzle

"Barstow, we're at the Raritan River and I'm famished! How far have we come since leaving Maplewood?"

"We've come half the distance from where we are now to Point Pleasant Beach, where we're going to have lunch at Dave's Seafood Shanty!"

Here we see Aunt Hattie out for a drive in her 1903 Benz Parsifal. She's headed for Atlantic City with her husband, Barstow, and their driver, Uncle Mohr. Later on, after lunch, a weary Aunt Hattie once again asked her husband where they were. "Well, Barstow, we've reached Forked River. How much further is it to Atlantic City?"

"Hattie, my answer to that is the same as the one that I gave to you at the Raritan River 76 miles ago!"

"Really, Barstow, if I'd known that the distance between Maplewood and Atlantic City was so far I'd have gone to Lake Hopatcong instead!"

From the above information can the reader calculate the total distance that Hattie had to travel to reach the fabled boardwalk at Atlantic City?

World's Trickiest "Archaeology" Puzzle

"Well, Petrie, what do you think of my hunch now? I told you that if we dug here we'd find the Tablet of the Scribes!"

"Quite right, Hawkings. If memory serves me correctly, the fledgling scribe had to place the above seven hieroglyphic symbols seven times within the Grid of Harmony. No individual symbol was to appear more than once in any one horizontal row or vertical column. Furthermore, they could not be repeated in either of the two great diagonals."

(The reader can take this test by using the letters "A" through "G" instead of trying to draw the symbols.)

World's Trickiest "Phrenology" Puzzle

"*Let me introduce myself. I am 'Phrenology Man,' the world's most successful quiz show contestant. I know all, see all, and, if the price is right, tell all. The following ten questions can all be answered with words starting with the letter 'L.' Let's see if you can equal the perfect score I made on my last show.*"

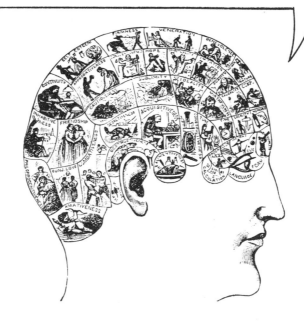

1. A sea monster.
2. Type of eel.
3. A male servant of low rank.
4. Tricks of a stage magician.
5. To beat soundly.
6. A quick, little old man.
7. Found between September 23 and October 21.
8. Turn-of-the-century drug.
9. Small tree-dwelling monkey.
10. An intricate network of winding passages.

World's Trickiest "Fencing" Puzzle

"Land sake, Emma, do you know what Zebediah is up to now? He wants to divide the fruit orchard with four straight fences so he can graze the horses there!"

"And that's not all! He says the four fences will create eleven enclosures and each enclosure will contain one apple tree. I know the fences can cross each other, but I can't figure out where they go. After these pies are done let's see if we can solve this problem!"

The reader is invited to grab a post hole digger and meet us down at the orchard.

World's Trickiest "Doggie" Puzzle

Here's a lost doggie that's really in trouble. Aunt Agatha's pet, Basil, has wandered away from home and become lost in the woods. Basil is so scared, he looks like a cubist's rendering of a canine. Can the reader help Basil get back home by cutting the drawing of him into two pieces and then reassembling them to form a square? Cut along the straight lines that make up the helpless pup.

World's Trickiest "WWII" Puzzle

"Babbington, I've just discovered the most amazing coincidence concerning World War II. If you add up the birth dates, ages in 1944, dates of taking power, and years in office of the five main leaders of the Western world, the sums of the numbers in 1944 are all the same!"

"If you're right, that's the greatest coincidence of all time! But surely there must be a rational explanation for this oddity?"

	Churchill	Roosevelt	Stalin	Hitler	Mussolini
Year of birth	1874	1882	1879	1889	1883
Age in 1944	70	62	65	55	61
Took office	1940	1933	1924	1933	1922
Years in office	4	11	20	11	22
Total	3,888	3,888	3,888	3,888	3,888

Can the reader explain this coincidence?

World's Trickiest "License" Puzzle

"Look, Mike, here comes Dr. Stall. He sure loves that old 1909 Ford Model T that belonged to his father!"

"I know. When my dad saw it yesterday he remarked on the license plate. He said that if you added two more 'ones' to the plate you could change the number on it into a person. Can you figure out how to do that one, Biff?"

World's Trickiest "Chess" Puzzle

> "And, really, the audacity of the young pup was just too much to bear! After I soundly thrashed him in four straight games he had the temerity to challenge me to a battle of chess problems. Well, I wasn't averse to relieving the insolent whelp of a few dollars, so I acquiesced with alacrity. Now, get this. The first problem he dared me to solve was the famous Knights Problem. You know, the one where you have to figure out the maximum number of knights you can place on a chessboard without any two being able to attack one another? That one cost the young scamp dearly!"

In case the reader has forgotten, a knight can move up or down the chessboard either two squares horizontally and one square vertically or one square horizontally and two squares vertically. With this in mind what do you think was Philip Fopingham's answer to this poser?

World's Trickiest "Mad Scientist" Puzzle

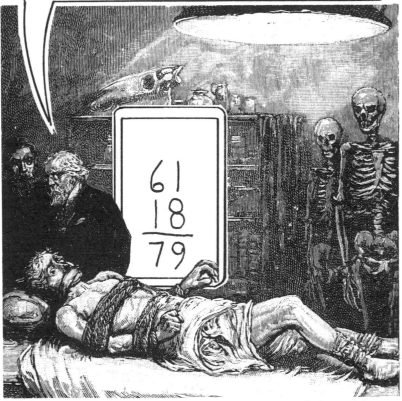

"This, Victor, is Claude Smythe, the cur that humiliated me before the faculty of Carfax University last night. In an attempt to discredit my theories, he openly challenged me to solve the trivial mathematical puzzle chalked on the board here behind me. To solve it, you must rearrange the four figures in the math problem so they equal 100. You can add plus or minus signs if you wish. I still haven't solved it, but who cares now? Soon Smythe will join my army of living skeletons. Victor, prepare my instruments. There's honest work to be done!"

$$\begin{array}{r} 61 \\ \underline{18} \\ 79 \end{array}$$

How could Professor Bentbrain have turned the tables on Smythe and solved this problem at the meeting?

World's Trickiest "Enchanted Vase" Puzzle

"One third of twelve if you divide,
By just one fifth of seven,
The true result (it has been tried)
Exactly is eleven."

Pictured here is the famous 19th-century French magician Charles De Vere. During a spirit séance De Vere is receiving a puzzle message from the great beyond. Can you help him solve this mysterious-sounding problem?

World's Trickiest "Substitution" Puzzle

The coming of the streetcar was quickly followed by a proliferation of traffic signs. Here we have the first recorded "Four Way Stop" sign. A local puzzle enthusiast drew a line under the word "WAY" and added a plus sign, turning the sign into a substitution problem. In case you're not familiar with this type of puzzle, you must substitute numbers 0 through 9 for the letters in the sign. The correct result is a correct addition problem. The same number must be used for each occurrence of the same letter.

World's Trickiest "Tea" Puzzle

Pictured above is Mr. Foo Ling Yu, the owner of the Spicy Tea Export Company. Mr. Yu was a great puzzler and enjoyed stumping the foreign agents who came to see him. He claimed that with a simple balance scale and four different iron weights he could weigh out any amount of tea in whole pounds, from one pound to 40 pounds. Can you determine the weight of each of these four weights and how Mr. Yu used them?

World's Trickiest "Circus" Puzzle

The above circus act is entitled "Splendiferous Stunts of Superlative Spelling." The ringmaster challenges the reader to make at least ten words that deal with the circus out of the 16 letters painted on the balls. You have until the Grand March begins to solve this one.

World's Trickiest "Hurdles" Puzzle

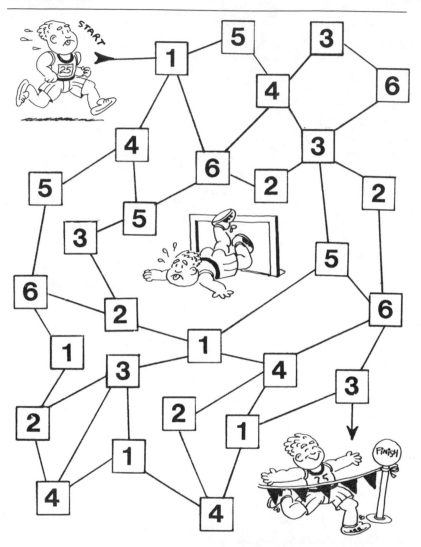

Welcome to the "Hurdle Maze" competition. To solve this event the runner must find the shortest route to the finish line over an even number of hurdles. The sum of the numbers on the hurdles jumped must be the greatest amount possible. Each square box represents a hurdle.

World's Trickiest "Clock" Puzzle

HOW MANY TIMES, IN A 24 HOUR PERIOD, DOES THE CLOCK "BIG BEN" STRIKE THREE TIMES IN SUCCESSION?

Back in 1887 the Puzzle Club of America was finally linked, ocean to ocean, with the latest Edison-improved ticker tape machines. Here we see Phineas Potts scanning a new puzzle coming into the club's New York office from Chicago. Let's see if we can help Potts send the correct answer back to the Windy City.

World's Trickiest "Gambling" Puzzle

Here we see an eastern dude being relieved of his spare change by that famous railroad cardsharp Poker Alice Ivers. When the pigeon tired of losing at poker, Alice would lay out 13 cards in a circle and bet him even money that she could beat him in a game of "Ring Around the Rosie." In this game each player, in turn, could remove from the circle one card or two cards next to one another. The player who picked up the last card was the winner. What was Alice's winning strategy in this so-called even-money game of chance?

World's Trickiest "Mental" Puzzle

31	18	10	27	14	31	18	10	27	14
12	24	16	28	20	12	24	16	28	20
13	30	22	9	26	13	30	22	9	26
19	11	23	15	32	19	11	23	15	32
25	17	29	21	8	25	17	29	21	8
31	18	10	27	14	31	18	10	27	14
12	24	16	28	20	12	24	16	28	20
13	30	22	9	26	13	30	22	9	26
19	11	23	15	32	19	11	23	15	32
25	17	29	21	8	25	17	29	21	8

When you've mastered this problem you'll be able to bill yourself as the "Mental Marvel."

Cut out a square of cardboard that is just large enough to cover four of the above-numbered squares. While your back is turned have someone place it on the chart so it covers four of the numbers. When you turn around and glance at the chart you are able to tell them instantly the sum of the four covered numbers. How is it done?

World's Trickiest "Checkerboard" Puzzle

Pop Bentley, owner of the "We Got It General Store!", came up with a new puzzle to beat Cy Corncrib with. He glued nine white checkers and a black king to a checkerboard and cut the board into eight pieces. He then challenged Cy to rearrange the eight pieces so that the king would be able to jump all nine white pieces in a single move. You have until planting time to solve this one.

World's Trickiest "Stone Carver" Puzzle

"Well, Popol, we're the only ones in our team to show up on the last day of this project. Do you know it's taken us as many months to finish this Calendar Stone as there are workers in our team!"

"You're right, Kuku. If we had had six more workers in our team we could have finished it in one month!"

From the information given in the above conversation can you figure out how many workers there were in the team?

World's Trickiest "Conundrum" Puzzles

"What is the most religious fish in the sea?"

"What has eight wheels but carries only one person?"

"In what country was the first doughnut found?"

"What part of London is found in France?"

"How did Jonah feel when the whale swallowed him?"

When the California Conundrum Club hit town in 1891 for the North American Puzzle Convention, they spent the day before the competition sightseeing along Fifth Avenue and honing their riddle-solving skills. Hop on and join in the fun!

World's Trickiest "Egg" Puzzle

Albert, the unchallenged prince of butlers, has done it again. For the second year in a row he is being honored by the Puzzle Club for submitting the winning gastronomic puzzle. His problem was: "How would you boil a fifteen-minute egg if you had only two sand timers, one that ran for 11 minutes and another that ran for 7 minutes, to time it with?" Once again Albert received a standing ovation and a glass of the bubbly for this one. The reader is invited to join the party and crack the problem before dessert is served.

World's Trickiest "Star" Puzzle

"All is now clear, Ludwig. Please place the first coin on circle number . . . !"

The mentalist, pictured here in another era, is about to solve the famous "Star of Salamanca" coin puzzle. The object is to place a coin on any empty numbered circle and then, moving along one of the lines, to pass over the next circle, and to then lay the coin on the next empty circle. Continue along in this fashion until all the circles, numbered 1 through 9, have been covered by coins.

World's Trickiest "Stirrer" Puzzle

"I tell you, Thelma, you missed all the excitement! An hour before you arrived, Boynton took Norbert for a cool $1,000 on a wager. He put nine cocktail stirrers down in front of Norbert and bet him he couldn't arrange them to form seven equilateral triangles. After 15 minutes Norbert wrote him a check and stormed out of the bar. Boynton's down at the bank trying to cash it now."

"I should get a commission. I was the one who showed the puzzle to Boynton!"

World's Trickiest "Underwater" Puzzle

"No, Miranda, her age is not 38. You must try harder. Remember, five years ago Mrs. Bellows was five times older than her daughter, Cecily. Now she is only three times as old as Cecily. What is Mrs. Bellows' age today?"

"38 years old?"

This has to be one of the strangest acts in the history of entertainment. Billed as Professor Nemo and Miranda, the Underwater Puzzlette, they toured North America and Europe answering every puzzle put to them from the audience. As Miranda could only surface between questions, she had to find the correct answers quickly and bubble them to the professor or face a watery end. Can you help her ascertain Mrs. Bellows' current age?

World's Trickiest "Wand" Puzzle

"Merlin challenges the reader to solve his famous 'Triangle Wand Puzzle.' Move three of the wands to new positions so that you are left with four equal-size triangles."

World's Trickiest "Poker" Puzzle

> "After this rubber let's take a break. I want to give Maynard a chance to win back his money at a little game of five-handed poker."

> "Good idea, Baldwin. Shall we bet even money again that you can't find five pat poker hands in any 25 cards I deal you after shuffling the deck?"

A pigeon like Maynard comes along all too infrequently. In this "game," the player who receives the twenty-five cards must arrange them into five pat poker hands. A pat poker hand is one with three-of-a-kind or better in it. Although this sounds like a tough thing to do, you can probably do it eight or nine times out of 10.

First, deal the cards face-up onto the table in five rows of five cards each. Then it's best to look for three-of-a-kinds first, then straights and flushes. You'll be surprised how easy it is to find five pat hands. The hard part is to find someone like Maynard to play with.

Another game is for both players to take 25 cards and each make up five pat hands. The contestants then bet on who has the most winning hands.

World's Trickiest "Quibble" Puzzle

Mike and his friends are researching a problem in the Puzzle Club library. Let's see if we can give them a hand.

World's Trickiest "Farm" Puzzle

> "Ebenezer, I'll trade you six pigs for a horse. You'll then have twice as many animals as I'll have."

> "Hold on, Zebediah. I'll trade you 14 sheep for a horse. You'll then have three times as many animals as I'll have."

> "I have a better idea. Absalom, I'll trade you four cows for a horse. You'll then have six times as many animals as I'll have."

ZEBEDIAH

EBENEZER

ABSALOM

Listening to these three horse traders, you should have enough information to figure out how many animals each of them now owns.

World's Trickiest "Planets" Puzzle

To commemorate the recent conjunction of the planets Venus, Earth, and Mars, Willard Starfinder, amateur astronomer and well-known puzzler, has posted the following problem on his bulletin board. He wrote the names of these planets in the form of a subtraction problem. Replace each letter with a number, using the same number for the same letter wherever it appears, so you end up with a valid mathematical expression. You have until the next conjunction to solve it.

World's Trickiest "Church Jumble" Puzzle

"But really, Mildred, I had every intention of taking you out to dinner tonight. Unfortunately I got carried away at the church's Jumble Sale today and spent every last cent I had. Here's what happened: I spent a dollar to get into the sale. Next I spent half of what I had left for a radio. I then spent $2.00 for a knockwurst sandwich. I then spent half what I had left for a picture of a windmill. Being still hungry, I bought a piece of boysenberry pie for $2.00. I then browsed through a stack of books, where I found an old Fred Fearnot story I had never read, and I purchased it for half of the money I had left. I next purchased a lemon ice for $2.00. While eating it I perused the odds-and-ends table, where I found a very nice comb that I bought for half of what I had left. By this time it was time to go. On the way out of the church I put my last dollar in the poor box and came straight over here."

"Cuthbert, if we ever get married—which seems doubtful—I'll manage the money. Now tell me how much money you originally took to the Jumble and how much you spent for each of the four items."

World's Trickiest "Card" Puzzle

> *"These four face-down cards contain all four suits and the values Ace, King, Queen, and Jack. Here are five clues that will help you figure out what each card is:*
>
> 1. *The Ace is to the right of the Spade.*
> 2. *The Diamond is to the left of the Queen.*
> 3. *The Club is to the right of the Queen.*
> 4. *The Heart is to the left of the Jack.*
> 5. *The Spade is to the right of the Jack.*

Mike Miller, along with Linda Kane and Biff Bennington, is shown here relaxing in the Puzzle Club's game room. Mike is challenging them to discover the values of the face-down cards he's just dealt out. The reader is invited to play along. For the sake of clarity, assume that the clues pertain to the cards as they face the reader.

World's Trickiest "Pyramid of Karnak" Puzzle

It is written that upon the return of Pharaoh Horemheb, after a great victory over the enemies of Egypt, the royal scribes commemorated the battle by creating the now-famous Pyramid Puzzle of Karnak. To solve this ancient problem you must rearrange the numbers one through nine so the total of the four numbers along any one side of the triangle will be 20.

World's Trickiest "Anagram" Puzzles

"Are you ready to order from Me a No Study, Sir?"

"Yes, Henri, tonight I'll start off with Man Take Loss and finish up with A Race Track, or I Sin."

"I'll start with a Dad Saw Floral and follow that with But Marge Has Tripe."

Fred and Alice are celebrating his promotion with a night out at the famous Anagram Club, where all the dishes are written as anagrams on the menu. Can you decode their orders? (Anagrams are words or groups of words where the letters have been mixed up to form new words. For example, the word "meals" could be made into the word "Salem.")

World's Trickiest "Train" Puzzle

No. 463.   NEW YORK, OCTOBER 18, 1907.   Price 5 Cents.

FRED FEARNOT AND RAILROAD JACK
OR, AFTER THE TRAIN WRECKERS
By HAL STANDISH

Fred Fearnot, hero of the dime novel, needs your help fast! Fred and his friends have captured the Train Wreckers Gang. Now he has to save the afternoon passenger train. He's too far away to flag down the work train just coming out of Dead Man's Tunnel. However, the daily passenger train is just entering the other end of the tunnel and is travelling at 75 miles per hour. The tunnel is one-half mile long. It will take 6 seconds for the train to completely enter the tunnel. If Fred runs his fastest he can reach the tunnel's exit in 27 seconds. Will this be fast enough for him to flag down either the engineer or the brakeman in the caboose?

World's Trickiest "Charade" Puzzle

The author is caught catnapping between problems. The first five lines of the verse he is dreaming about give clues to the spelling of a word. The last line supplies a final hint.

World's Trickiest "Word Pyramid" Puzzle

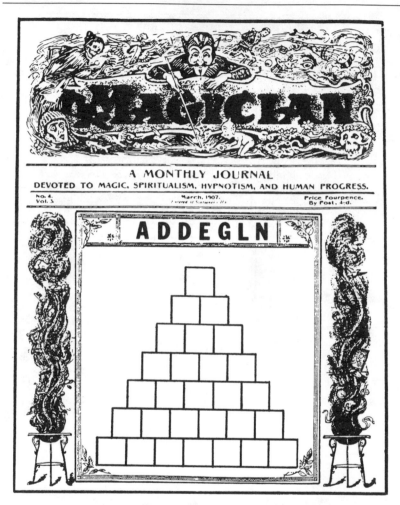

A MONTHLY JOURNAL

DEVOTED TO MAGIC, SPIRITUALISM, HYPNOTISM, AND HUMAN PROGRESS.

No. 4.
Vol. 3.

March, 1907.

Price Fourpence.
By Post, 4½d.

ADDEGLN

The year is 1907 and Will Goldston, editor of *Magician,* a monthly journal, is challenging his readers to solve a "Word Pyramid" puzzle. Using the seven letters A D D E G L N, you must form seven words, starting with a one-letter word at the top of the pyramid. Each subsequent word, going down, must use all of the letters in the preceding word plus one new letter.

World's Trickiest "Spy" Puzzle

Over 90 years ago two spies met briefly at a costume ball at the Hotel Intrigue in London. Lucretia whispered "Fly for your life!" They were both caught sneaking out of the hotel. Later, in his cell, Ludwick, who was a great puzzler, concocted a problem out of Lucretia's warning. First he wrote "Fly for your life" as an addition problem. Then to solve it he tried to substitute numbers for the letters. The same number had to be given to each occurrence of the same letter. (Hint: I = 1 and O = zero.)

World's Trickiest "Q" Puzzle

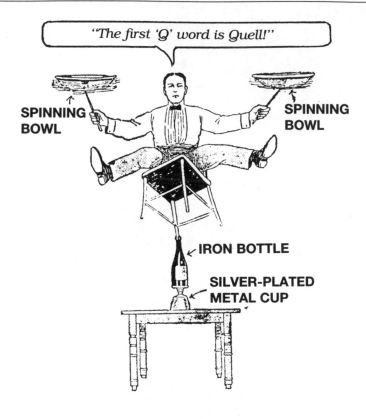

"The first 'Q' word is Quell!"

SPINNING BOWL

SPINNING BOWL

IRON BOTTLE

SILVER-PLATED METAL CUP

Waldo Quackenbush, noted society juggler, has added a new twist to his act. While balancing on his precarious perch he answers all puzzles put to him. The one he is pictured here working on is the famous "Q" puzzle. To solve it, he must find five-letter synonyms that begin with the letter "Q," for the 20 words listed below. Waldo has found the first one. Can you help him with the other nineteen?

1. subdue   6. nimble   11. swallow   16. secluded
2. pen   7. repeat   12. scruple   17. tremble
3. measure   8. doubt   13. seeming   18. monarch
4. share   9. game bird 14. entirely   19. twist
5. line   10. singular 15. search   20. oddities

World's Trickiest "Circle" Puzzle

Zeppo the clown, a fool of renown, has a problem I'm sure you'll like. In our picture we find him balanced on top of two barrels. The barrels are shown in outline for a reason. Cut these two barrels into four equal pieces of the same size and shape. (You will cut each barrel into two pieces.) Now, the fun begins. Rearrange these four pieces into a perfect circle.

Try to finish before Tamara the Tiger finishes off Zeppo.

World's Trickiest "Poem" Puzzle

"Really, Lionel, I'm most disappointed. You should have solved my little puzzle in a thrice. Now stop your pouting and listen carefully to every word I say:

> The beginning of eternity,
> The end of time and space,
> The beginning of every end,
> The end of every place."

Now, what is this little poem all about?

World's Trickiest "1995" Puzzle

Mike Miller and his friends are shown here arriving for the 1995 Puzzle Convention. The kickoff puzzle deals with the digits of the date: 1, 9, 9, and 5. The contestants must set down these digits, in the order given, along with the signs for addition, subtraction, division, multiplication and square root, to form math expressions equal to 1 through 10. For example:

$$(1 \times (\sqrt{9} + \sqrt{9})) - 5 = 1$$

You have 45 minutes to find the other nine expressions.

World's Trickiest "Fours" Puzzle

Professor Flunkum's students know that if they chalk an interesting problem on the wall outside his study window he's apt to get so caught up in it that he'll miss his classes. Right now he's trying to figure out how to arrange five fours and one plus sign so the result equals 55. If you figure it out, don't tell the professor. His students are hard on snitches.

World's Trickiest "Hippo" Puzzle

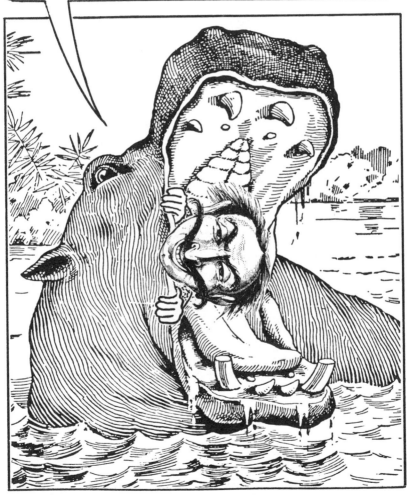

"Er, excuse me, but I've gotten myself in a bit of a pickle. My foot seems to be jammed behind a tonsil or something. However, If you could get me out of here I'd be most grateful. Why, I'll even tell you how to make the number 7 even. Now, that's even better than money, isn't it? Wait, don't go away! I'll throw in an anagram too."

How do you make 7 even, anyway?

World's Trickiest "Balloonist" Puzzle

"Well, Mr. Ramsgate, it seems I'll have a bit of a wait until the rescue chaps get here. Let's match puzzles! The other day I heard of a Russian man who had three sons. The first son, Rab, was a lawyer. The second son, Ymra, was a soldier, and the third son was a sailor. From these facts can you tell what the third son's name was?"

"That's a nifty problem, Mr. Wainwright. While I'm cogitating over it, see if you can figure out what plant stands for the number 4!"

The above just goes to show that you can't keep a good puzzler down or, in this case, up.

World's Trickiest "Store" Puzzle

> *"Let's see now. I have a dollar to spend and I think I'll purchase an assortment of colored thread. First, give me some two-cent blue spools. Next, I'll take ten times as many one-cent red spools as I took blue spools. Finally, I'll take the balance of my money in five-cent green spools. And please hurry! My carriage is double-parked at the curb!"*

THE LITTLE STOREKEEPER'S OUTFIT, WITH CASH CARRIER

It's Christmas time in 1902 and the Bartholomew kids have received a Franklin Play Store set complete with toy money, products to sell and an overhead cash carrier. Neville is in charge of making change while Bascomb waits on his sister, Fleurette. Back in those days a dollar went a long way, no pun intended. Can you figure out just how many spools of each type of thread were purchased during the above transaction?

World's Trickiest "Automaton" Puzzle

The Victorian automaton, "Psycho," is attempting to solve the famous "Ten-Digit Number" problem. In the first box, place a digit that is equal to the number of zeroes in the whole number. In the second box, place a digit equal to the number of ones in the number. Continue in this manner until you've filled in the complete ten-digit number.

World's Trickiest "Subtraction" Puzzle

"Now who wrote this subtraction problem on the mirror? I know it's wrong, but the Mad Hatter insists I'm looking at it the wrong way. He says that if I study it from the correct angle it will be perfectly correct. I know he's in this mirror somewhere but I just can't find him. This just gets curiouser and curiouser."

Can you help Alice find the solution to this problem so she'll be one up on the Mad Hatter?

World's Trickiest "Balancing Card" Puzzle

"The following small item is one that has won me many a pint of ale over the years. When someone is anxious to make a wager with you, hand him a playing card and challenge him to balance it upright along one of the long edges of the card. Specify that the card must remain upright, in the center of the table, for at least five seconds. Nothing else must touch the card in any way."

A lesson in card betting from that famous magician of the early 1800s, Professor Anderson, the wizard of the North.

World's Trickiest "Contest" Riddles

> *"What is full of holes and still holds water?"*
>
> *"Where did Noah keep his bees?"*
>
> *"What has five eyes, but cannot see?"*
>
> *"When is a doctor most annoyed?"*

The time is May, 1926. The place is the offices of England's premier magic magazine, *The Magic Wand*, and the editor, George Johnson, and his friends are having a riddle contest. Let's listen in!

World's Trickiest "Party" Puzzle

The Bank Note Maker. This machine will turn sheets of plain paper into bank notes. 1/9

Water on the Brain. This ingenious piece of apparatus produces a quantity of water from any person's forehead.

A Quaint Telescope. The telescope is supposed to contain a number of pictures which move when the outside case of the telescope is turned round. Having announced what the pictures are, you will have no difficulty in finding some one who would like to see them. He puts the telescope to his eyes and unknown to himself, has a black eye before he has finished with the telescope.

The Spray Flower

A group of partygoers on their way to a puzzle and joke soiree stopped off at the local magic store to purchase some game prizes. Each purchased one item. Each item cost the same price, which was between $1.00 and $4.00, and the price contained an even number of cents. The total amount spent by the group, before taxes, was $20.30. How many people were in the group and how much did each item cost?

ANSWERS

"Checkers" Puzzle (page 6). Mr. Fogg's winning moves were: 7 to 10, 15 to 6, and 4 to 8. The white checkers were then locked in and couldn't make a move, thereby giving the game to the black side.

"Joan Crawford" Puzzle (page 7). The only word that answers the test question is *sexton*. A sexton is a church official in charge of maintaining the church and church property. He sometimes rings the bells and, in days gone by, he also dug the graves.

"Stereoscope" Puzzle (page 8). Starting at the upper left part of the picture, you'll find that 1) the bird is missing from the wall torch, 2) one of the juggling balls is missing, 3) the king's drinking cup has disappeared from his right hand, 4) the left candle on the wall is out, 5) the troubadour's lute is missing its strings, 6) the troubadour's left shoe is missing, 7) the shadow cast by the troubadour's right leg is missing. Starting at the lower left of the picture, 8) the dog's dog-tag is missing, 9) no wine is coming out of the jug, 10) the man on the right edge of the picture has lost his moustache, and 11) the man at the top of the table has lost the wafer in his right hand.

"Ladder" Puzzles (page 10). 1) SICK, SILK, SILL, SELL, WELL; 2) BIRD, BIND, BEND, BENT, BEST, NEST; 3) PIG, WIG, WAG, WAY, SAY, STY; 4) MINE, MINT, MIST, MOST, MOAT, COAT, COAL; 5) CITY, CITE, MITE, MATE, FATE, FARE, FARM.

"Dragon" Puzzle (page 11). The answers to the dragon's puzzles are: 1) "Tarzan Strips Forever!" 2) You make a hippopotamus float with a large glass and a lot of root beer. 3) When spelling the numbers in the given series, each number is spelled with one more letter than the last: 1 = one; 4 = four; and 3 = three. Therefore, the next number in the series should be spelled with six letters. That number, in ascending numeric order, would be 11 (eleven).

"Tea Chest" Puzzle (page 12). In this example, to construct the Enchanted Tea Chest use six pieces of Bristol board 2½″ × 3½″ (Fig. 1). Crease and fold the two narrow ends, as indicated by the dashes, to form flaps A and B. After all six pieces have been folded in this manner, place one of them on the table, flap-side-up. Next, take two more pieces and slip their ends under the piece on the table (Fig. 2). Hold these two pieces up with one hand while taking the next two cards and slipping their plain edges down inside flaps A and B of the bottom piece. You have now formed the other two sides of the box (Fig. 3). Turn the flaps of these last two pieces around C and D of the pieces shown in Fig. 2.

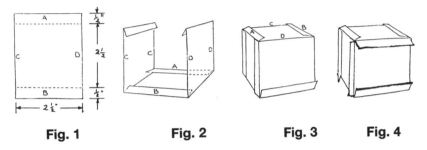

Fig. 1   **Fig. 2**   **Fig. 3**   **Fig. 4**

Now for the top of the box. Take the final piece and, with the flaps facing down, place it on top of the construction in Fig. 3. You should now have a box that looks like the one pictured in Fig. 4. Tighten the box by pressing all of the flaps down against the sides. The box can now be tossed about without fear of its coming apart.

Entertain your friends by exhibiting the assembled box, taking it apart, and challenging them to put it back together again. Also, paste holiday wrapping paper over the six pieces to create a colorful and unusual puzzle.

"Restaurant" Puzzle (page 13). Ten people sat down to lunch. Each one's share of the $80.00 check was $8.00. After the Benson twins skipped out, leaving eight diners, those remaining had to add $2.00 each to their share to cover the balance. Thus, each of the eight paid $10.00.

"Quotation" Puzzle (page 14). Starting with the "A" at the lower left side of the picture, read around the frame counterclockwise. The famous quotation that Mata Hari used was from *She Stoops to Conquer,* a play by Oliver Goldsmith, and reads, "Ask me no questions, and I'll tell you no fibs."

"Kite" Puzzle (page 15). You'll find a total of 31 equilateral triangles contained in the construction of Mr. Okito's kite. Broken down they are:

1. 16 small triangles
2. 7 triangles made up of 4 smaller ones
3. 3 triangles made up of 9 smaller ones
4. 4 triangles made up of 16 smaller ones
5. 1 large outer triangle.

The hardest of the triangles to find is the seventh one, made up of four smaller triangles. You'll find it in the center of the kite with the three points of the triangle touching the centers of the lines that make up the inner triangle that is composed of 16 smaller triangles.

"Hidden Word" Puzzles (page 16). The locale of the top picture is Colorado. "Did you ever see such a <u>color</u>?" "A <u>d</u>ownright brick red, isn't it."

The second place is Athens, Georgia, that is. "<u>Pa then</u> <u>s</u>aw Esau kissing Kate."

We are indebted to Sam Loyd, America's greatest puzzler, for these two turn-of-the-century gems.

"Sledding" Puzzle (page 17). It took Harry and Harriet four minutes to finish the mile, while the Brodys covered the course in 10 minutes, a difference of six minutes. Thus, Harry's sled was two and a half times faster than the Brodys'.

"Bow Tie" Puzzle (page 18). (See drawing.)

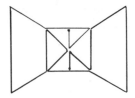

"Stick" Puzzle (page 19). The following drawing tells all. And remember, we didn't specify that the six squares all had to be the same size. (See drawing.)

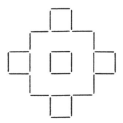

"Famous Sayings" Puzzle (page 20). It's doubtful if either of these famous gentlemen ever uttered the sayings attributed to them. However, the one thing the sayings have in common is that they are both palindromes. That is, the sentences are the same when read backward or forward. Another example is "Madam, I'm Adam."

"Riddle" Puzzles (page 21). 1) Wheeling West Virginia; 2) the baby is a little bigger; 3) when it is adrift; 4) because it doesn't run long without winding.

"Diner" Puzzle (page 22). "Stir two! Wheat!" is a plate of scrambled eggs with whole wheat toast. Below is one way to solve this problem:

$$
\begin{array}{r}
9\ 7\ 5\ 4 \\
7\ 1\ 3 \\
\hline
1\ 0\ 4\ 6\ 7
\end{array}
$$

"Golf Tees" Puzzle (page 23). The following drawing shows how Nelda formed four perfect squares with 24 golf tees to win a new set of irons from MacDivot. (See drawing.)

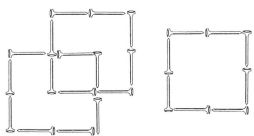

107

"Word Square" Puzzle (page 24). (See drawing.)

"Match Stick" Puzzle (page 25). The following drawing shows how the 14 matches are laid out to form five diamond figures all the same size and shape. (See drawing.)

"Puzzle Spy" Puzzle (page 26). The answer that came over the Snooper Phone was, <u>UNDERGROUND</u>. As for the hint, in London they call the <u>subway</u> the <u>underground</u>.

"Word" Puzzle (page 27). The four words each contain three consecutive letters that appear in reverse alphabetical order: <u>FED</u>ORA, U<u>PON</u>, SPR<u>OU</u>TS, JI<u>HA</u>D.

"Cloth" Puzzle (page 28). The solution to the draper's puzzle is to lay out the square of cloth and cut it twice along lines *A–A* and *B–B*. These lines are drawn from a point one-third up and one-third across on the sides of the square where they intersect. You are then left with squares *1* and *2*. The third square is created by taking pieces *3* and *4* and sewing them together along their long edges. This forms a square that is equal in size to square *2*.

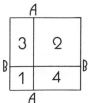

"Beheading" Puzzle (page 29). 1) arise, rise; 2) close, lose; 3) scold, cold; 4) tray, ray; 5) Grail, rail; 6) tram, ram; 7) drum, rum; 8) sloop, loop.

"Betting" Puzzle (page 30). Two-thirds of three-quarters is always equal to one half of any given amount.

$$(2/3 \times 3/4) \times \$111.00 =$$
$$6/12 \times \$111.00 =$$
$$1/2 \times \$111.00 = \$55.50$$

"Telephone" Puzzle (page 31). In the new family there were four boys and three girls.

"Ports of Call" Puzzle (page 32).
EASGILR = ALGIERS (Algeria)
CSIANIO = NICOSIA (Cyprus)
LASNEP = NAPLES (Italy)
RHOTCNI = CORINTH (Greece)
CVALIENA = VALENCIA (Spain)
UNASLIBT = ISTANBUL (Turkey)
NUOTOL = TOULON (France)
RDLAEXAIAN = ALEXANDRIA (Egypt)
UYERSCAS = SYRACUSE (Sicily)
ZNIGABEH = BENGHAZI (Libya)

"Bar Room" Puzzle (page 33). The six coins that would get you one on the house are: one half dollar, one quarter and four dimes.

"Money" Puzzle (page 34). The mayor started out with $8.75 in his pocket. The hat clerk lent him $8.75, giving him $17.50. After paying $10.00 for the hat, he then had $7.50 in his pocket. Next, the suit salesman lent him $7.50, giving him $15.00. After paying $10.00 for the jacket he then was left with $5.00. Finally, the shoe salesman lent him $5.00, giving him $10.00 which he used to pay for the shoes. This left the mayor nicely outfitted but as broke as last election's promises.

"Rebus" Puzzle (page 35). The first message, fully decoded, reads: "Captain Forbes arrived in the West Indies today with his forces."

The second message reads: "Captain Forbes mission a bust. He ran backward and forward across the island like a stranger in paradise, finding no one."

If you cracked those codes, you may be CIA material.

"Nails" Puzzle (page 36). This problem has seven correct answers. If you move any one of the seven interior nails (those marked with an "X") to the empty position in the center bottom row of nails, you will then have a layout that contains four small squares (each made up of four nails) and two large squares (each made up of eight nails).

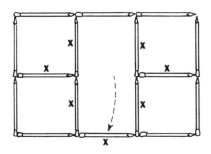

"Weighing" Puzzle (page 37). Here's how Linda and Mike solved Professor Kane's problem. First they divided the nine weights into three piles of three weights each. They then put two of these piles on the scale, one pile on each side. If either of the piles went up in the air, then that pile must contain the light weight. If they balanced evenly then the third pile had to contain the light weight. Either way, after the first weighing, Mike and Linda knew which pile contained the light weight. For the second weighing they selected two of the coins from the light group and placed one on each side of the scales. If the scales balanced, then the third coin was the light one; otherwise the coin on the side of the scales that went up was the coin they were looking for. Either way, Mike and Linda solved the puzzle in two weighings.

"Fishing" Puzzle (page 38). Our fishing fools chalked up the following totals for the day: Emmet = 4 fish, Calvin = 3 fish, Quentin = 2 fish, and Wylie = 1 fish.

"Poor Sport" Puzzle (page 39). The first word is AN-TIPERSPIR<u>ANT</u>. The second is TORMEN<u>TOR</u>.

"Sport" Puzzle (page 40). The 12 sports employing a solid hardball that Norma conquered that summer were: 1) Baseball; 2) billiards; 3) bocce; 4) bowling; 5) cricket; 6) croquet; 7) field hockey; 8) golf; 9) handball; 10) lacrosse; 11) pocket billiards; 12) polo.

"What" Puzzles (page 41). 1) A cat has claws at the tip of its paws; a comma has its pause at the end of a clause. 2) The letter "A," because it makes *her hear*. 3) DK (decay). 4) Bacon. 5) X-P-D-N-C (expediency).

"Toy Train" Puzzle (page 42). The sixteen individual moves are as follows: 1 to 5, 3 to 7, 7 to 1, 8 to 4, 4 to 3, 3 to 7, 6 to 2, 2 to 8, 8 to 4, 4 to 3, 5 to 6, 6 to 2, 2 to 8, 1 to 5, 5 to 6, and 7 to 1.

"Legacy" Puzzle (page 43). After looking over the will, Judge Fineum said, "What the deceased had in mind was that if Reggie should arrive at the house first, then he should get twice as much of the estate as his mother. Secondly, if his brother Farnsworth should arrive first then the mother was to get twice as much as Farnsworth. In either case the son who arrived second was to get nothing. However, since they both arrived at exactly the same time, I suggested that we divide the estate into seven parts and divide it accordingly: Reggie would get four parts, the mother two parts and Farnsworth one part. This would be an equitable division of the estate that would follow the stipulations outlined in the will. Everyone went away more or less happy."

"Doodle Art" Puzzles (page 44). The first picture depicts an army officer, swagger stick tucked under his arm, walking into his house with his dog. The second picture is an early rebus and reads, "Be independent, but not too independent." The "B" is in the "D" and is pendant. The cigarette is a "butt" and the "2" is in the "D" and is pendant.

"Quilting" Puzzle (page 45). Sam Loyd listed 17 names in his original presentation of this puzzle. To date, we have been able to find 35 names. There may be, and probably are, more. However, readers able to come up with twenty or more names have solved this puzzle admirably. My listing is as follows: Ann, Anna, Annie, Cary, Cindi, Diana, Diane, Dinah, Edna, Enid, Ina, Jane, Janel, Jean, Jenny, Judy, Jule, Lea, Lena, Mae, Maia, Mary, Maud, Minna, Minnie, Minny, Nan, Nana, Nancy, Nina, Rae, Raina, Rana, Rania, Rue.

"Note" Puzzle (page 46). Algernon's note to his bookmaker reads as follows: "Sir, between friends, I understand your overbearing disposition; a man even with the world is above contempt, whilst the ambitious are beneath ridicule."

I take it that the man even with the world was Algernon after paying off his debt, while the ambitious man beneath ridicule was the bookmaker who was always hounding him. Unfortunately for Algernon, I'm sure fate soon set him back where he was less than even with the world.

"Maze" Puzzle (page 47). The following route will quickly take you to Rosamond's bower. (See drawing.)

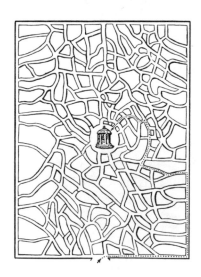

"Candle" Puzzle (page 48). As it turned out, the reverend made short work of the sexton's puzzle. The candles to be moved are indicated by the broken lines in the drawing below. (See drawing.)

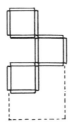

"Triangle" Puzzle (page 50). There are 29 triangles in the rug design Biff challenged Mike to solve. We've labelled the points in the design 1 through 9. Below are listed the three points associated with each of these triangles. (See drawing.)

125	137	235	279	459
127	139	236	289	468
128	145	237	349	357
567	129	159	239	359
579	134	178	256	367
789	135	179	257	

"Square" Puzzle (page 49). Consider that the smallest square is one unit wide by one unit high. There are 64 of these squares. Next, we have squares that are two units by two units. There are 49 of these squares. The breakdown is as follows:

$$1 \times 1 = 64$$
$$2 \times 2 = 49$$
$$3 \times 3 = 36$$
$$4 \times 4 = 25$$
$$5 \times 5 = 16$$
$$6 \times 6 = 9$$
$$7 \times 7 = 4$$
$$8 \times 8 = 1$$

Total = 204 squares

"Vowel" Puzzle (page 51). In the following drawing, the heavy lines denote the edges of the five pieces. Each piece contains the letters "A," "E," "I," "O" and "U." (See drawing.)

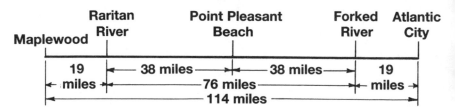

"Wager" Puzzle (page 52). Biff said you'd be left with four pieces . . . and he lost. The answer is three pieces, regardless of which way you cut the packet in two.

"Motoring" Puzzle (page 53). Aunt Hattie travelled 114 miles to reach Atlantic City. The following diagram tells all. (See drawing.)

"Archaeology" Puzzle (page 54). The answer that Hawkings and Petrie came up with is pictured below. (See drawing.)

a	b	c	d	e	f	g
d	e	f	g	a	b	c
g	a	b	c	d	e	f
c	d	e	f	g	a	b
f	g	a	b	c	d	e
b	c	d	e	f	g	a
e	f	g	a	b	c	d

"Phrenology" Puzzle (page 55). 1) Leviathan; 2) lamprey; 3) lackey; 4) legerdemain; 5) lambaste; 6) leprechaun; 7) Libra (zodiacal sign); 8) laudanum; 9) lemur; 10) labyrinth.

"Fencing" Puzzle (page 56). The following drawing shows Zebediah's solution to this grazing problem. (See drawing.)

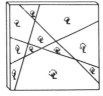

"Doggie" Puzzle (page 57). Here's how to return Basil to his own backyard. Cut along the heavy lines in figure 1, below. Take the right-hand piece, rotate it clockwise 90 degrees, and fit it up against the left-hand piece. You will now have a happy Basil back in his own yard looking out at the world through the front gate. (See drawings.)

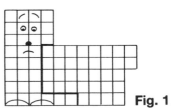

Fig. 1

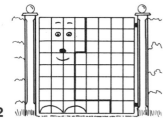

Fig. 2

"WWII" Puzzle (page 58). This only appears to be a co-incidence. The year in question is 1944. If we take the birthday of anyone born before 1944 and add the person's age to the year of birth, the result will always be 1,944. So, if we take the year a political figure entered office and add the number of years the figure served to this number—once again, only up to 1944—the total will be 1,944. Adding these two totals together gives 3,888, the totals in the chart. Try making up your own "coincidence" charts using world leaders of today.

"License" Puzzle (page 59). The first "one" goes across the first two "ones" in the license plate to form the letter "H." The second "one" goes up against the "3," forming the letter "B." The plate now reads "HOBO," a type of old-time tramp.

HOBO

"Chess" Puzzle (page 60). The total number of knights that can be placed on the board without any two being able to attack one another is 24. The following drawing shows their placement. (See drawing.)

"Mad Scientist" Puzzle (page 61). He could have turned the tables on Smythe by . . . turning the chalkboard upside down. The numbers are now in a new arrangement giving us the expression 81 plus 19, which equals 100. (See drawing.)

"Enchanted Vase" Puzzle (page 62). This is another one of those problems that makes use of Roman numerals. To start, one-third of TWELVE would be the letters LV, which in Roman numerals equals 55. Next, one-fifth of SEVEN would be the letter V, which in Roman numerals is equal to 5. Thus, 55 divided by 5 equals 11, as stated by the genie of the vase.

"Substitution" Puzzle (page 63).

$$
\begin{array}{r}
1\ 9\ 5\ 6 \\
+\quad 8\ 3\ 4 \\
\hline
2\ 7\ 9\ 0
\end{array}
$$

"Tea" Puzzle (page 64). The four weights were 1 pound, 3 pounds, 9 pounds, and 27 pounds. Fu Ling Yu would sometimes have to put weights on both sides of the scale when weighing out certain amounts. Some examples are:

	Left side of scale	Right side of scale
7 lbs. =	1 + 9	3 + 7 lbs. of tea
12 lbs. =	3 + 9	12 lbs. of tea
15 lbs. =	27	9 + 3 + 15 lbs. of tea
20 lbs. =	27 + 3	1 + 9 + 20 lbs. of tea

"Circus" Puzzle (page 65). The ringmaster came up with 16 circus-related words. If you can find more, you're eligible for top billing. Here's what he found: acrobat; balance; band; bear; beast; cage; clown; dancer; dogs; giant; lion; net; ring; seal; tent; and tiger.

"Hurdles" Puzzle (page 66). The shortest route over an even number of hurdles is twelve hurdles. Since there is more than one route using twelve hurdles, we must find the one with the largest number total. That total is 36, and the route is indicated below by following the dotted line. (See drawing.)

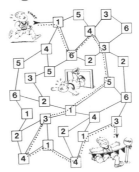

"Clock" Puzzle (page 67). Big Ben strikes three times in succession four times a day. The times are: 3 a.m.; 3 p.m.; 12:30, 1, and 1:30 a.m.; and 12:30, 1, and 1:30 p.m. Implicit in the question is the grouping of three strikes of the clock in a given period. Not specified was the stipulation that the intervals between strikes had to be of the same duration. In the first two cases, 3 a.m. and 3 p.m., the interval between strikes was about one second. In the second two cases the interval between strikes was 30 minutes. Still, all four occurrences fulfill the problem as presented on the ticker tape.

"Gambling" Puzzle (page 68). The player who goes second can be a sure winner if he, or she, knows the secret. Here it is: If the pigeon goes first and removes one card, the sharper removes two cards. If the pigeon removes two cards, the sharper removes one card. In either case, when the sharper removes his card(s), he makes sure the circle is divided into equal semi-circles each containing five cards. From that point on, the sharper removes from the opposite semi-circle the same number of cards the pigeon removes. This way, the sharper always takes up the last card and wins the bet.

When the sharper goes first, he removes just one card from the circle and waits for the opportunity to divide the cards in the circle into two contiguous sections, each section containing the same number of cards. With a little practice the sharper should be able to win 8, 9 or even 10 times out of 10 games. Unless, of course, he runs up against another player who is in the know. When this happens it's best to change trains and look for greener pastures. (See drawing.)

"Mental" Puzzle (page 69). This is one trick you can do over and over again without fear of revealing the secret. The following example provides the modus operandi. In the chart below, we've darkened the squares that contain the numbers 8, 25, 14 and 31. The sum of these numbers is 78. These numbers would be covered by the small cardboard square. Now, if you move diagonally by two spaces from any of the corners of this small square, the second small square you come to will contain the number 22. (These small squares that are two diagonal spaces away are called key numbers. We've circled them in our example.) Take the key number and subtract it from 100. You get 78, the sum of the four covered numbers. That's all you have to do to discover the sum of any covered four numbers on the chart. Regardless of where the four covered numbers are located on the chart, you will always be able to see at least one of the diagonal key numbers. (See drawing.)

"Checkerboard" Puzzle (page 70). In the drawing below we've rearranged and renumbered the squares in the solution to make it easier to give you the jumps in the winning move. Black jumps 8 to 15, 15 to 24, 24 to 31, 31 to 22, 22 to 15, 15 to 6, 6 to 13, 13 to 22, and 22 to 29. (See drawing.)

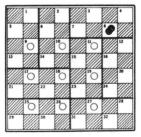

"Stone Carver" Puzzle (page 71). The stone-carving team totalled three sculptors at full strength. If three can carve a calendar in three months, one can carve it in nine months, and nine can carve it in one month.

"Conundrum" Puzzles (page 72). 1) The holy mackerel; 2) old-fashioned roller skates; 3) Greece (grease); 4) the letter "N"; 5) down in the mouth.

"Egg" Puzzle (page 73). When the water boiled, Albert dropped the egg in and turned both sand timers over. After the sand in the seven-minute timer ran out he turned it over once again. At this point, four minutes of sand was left in the 11-minute timer. When the sand in the 11-minute timer ran out, four minutes of sand was in the *bottom* of the 7-minute timer. Albert turned this timer over and when the sand in it ran out, a full 15 minutes had passed and he removed the egg from the water.

"Star" Puzzle (page 74). The following nine moves will win the day. The first position is where the coin is originally placed. The second is where it ends up after hopping the intervening circle: 2 to 4; 8 to 2; 5 to 8; 3 to 5; 9 to 3; 7 to 9; 1 to 7; 6 to 1; and 10 to 6. (See drawing.)

"Stirrer" Puzzle (page 75). Where there are stirrers, there are olives, and these are needed to solve this problem. First, take three stirrers and three olives and use them to form one equilateral triangle. The stirrers are stuck in the olives to hold the construction together. Lay the triangle on the bar and stick three more stirrers in the three olives. Tilt them so that they come together at the top, forming a pyramid. Cap the ends with another olive. You now have a four-sided triangle made up of equilateral triangles. Next, tilt the construction over onto one of its sides and, using the last three stirrers, build another pyramid and cap it with an olive. You now have a structure that is composed of seven equilateral triangles.

It's best to use extra-large olives when solving this puzzle. (See drawing.)

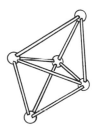

"Underwater" Puzzle (page 76). Mrs. Bellows is 30 years old and her daughter, Cecily, is 10. Today, Mrs. Bellows is three times as old as her daughter. Five years ago, when she was 25 and Cecily was 5, she was five times as old as her daughter.

"Wand" Puzzle (page 77). Three of the wands are removed from the original setup and reassembled to form a single new triangle. (See drawing.)

"Quibble" Puzzle (page 79). A "quibble" puzzle is usually one that has a tricky solution. That's the case with this one. To solve it, when you add the 2 to 191 you first draw a line under the 1 on the right and then you put the 2 under it. The number now reads 19½, which, of course, is less than 20. In other words, when you added the 2 to the 191 you just didn't sum the two figures together. Now you know what "quibbles" are all about!

"Farm" Puzzle (page 80). Zebediah has 11 animals, Ebenezer has 7 animals and Absalom has 21 animals.

"Planets" Puzzle (page 81). Here's the answer that Willard came up with.

$$\begin{array}{r} 5\ 4\ 7\ 3\ 9 \\ -\ 4\ 6\ 1\ 2\ 0 \\ \hline 8\ 6\ 1\ 9 \end{array}$$

"Church Jumble" Puzzle (page 82). Young and hapless, Cuthbert went to the Jumble with exactly $45 in his pockets. The radio cost him $22; the picture cost $10; the book went for $4; and the pocket comb set him back $1. The way to solve this problem is to work backwards from the dollar he put in the poor box as he left.

"Card" Puzzle (page 83). The four face-down cards, left to right, are King of Hearts, Jack of Diamonds, Queen of Spades and Ace of Clubs. (See drawing.)

"Pyramid of Karnak" Puzzle (page 84). The following drawing shows one solution to this puzzle. (See drawing.)

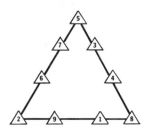

"Anagram" Puzzles (page 85). First off, let me say that this is not an Italian anagram club although Henri asked them if they were ready to order from *Today's Menu*. Fred's order should read *Salmon Steak* and *Carrot Raisin Cake*. Alice's order should read *Waldorf Salad* and *Hamburger Patties*. After that puzzle you're allowed a five-minute trip to the refrigerator before going on to the next problem.

"Train" Puzzle (page 86). At 75 miles per hour the passenger train can travel one-half mile in 24 seconds. (There are 3,600 seconds in an hour. Divided by 75 miles per hour, we get 48 seconds for the train to travel one mile. Thus a half-mile can be travelled in 24 seconds.) This means that the engine will emerge from the tunnel three seconds before Fred reaches the exit, too late for him to catch the engineer's eye. However, since it took six seconds for the train to completely enter the tunnel it will take six seconds before the last car, the caboose, will exit from it. This makes a total of 30 seconds from the time Fred started running towards the tunnel exit. Since Fred could reach the exit in 27 seconds he had three seconds to spare, long enough to catch the brakeman's attention and save the train.

"Charade" Puzzle (page 87). The word that the six clues point to is . . . EBONY. Each of the first five clues refers to *letters* in words.

"Word Pyramid" Puzzle (page 88). In puzzles of this type there is usually more than one solution. We give the following solution, starting at the top word and working down: A, LA, ALE, GALE, ANGLE, DANGLE, and GLADDEN.

"Spy" Puzzle (page 89). The following is Ludwick's solution to this problem. There may be others.

$$\begin{array}{r} 5\ 9\ 8 \\ 5\ 0\ 7 \\ +\ 8\ 0\ 4\ 7 \\ \hline 9\ 1\ 5\ 2 \end{array}$$

"Q" Puzzles (page 90).

1) Quell	6) Quick	11) Quaff	16) Quiet
2) Quill	7) Quote	12) Qualm	17) Quake
3) Quart	8) Query	13) Quasi	18) Queen
4) Quota	9) Quail	14) Quite	19) Quirk
5) Queue	10) Queer	15) Quest	20) Quips

"Circle" Puzzle (page 91). Cut the barrel outlines along the dotted lines as shown in Figure 1. Rearrange the four pieces as shown in Figure 2. (See drawings.)

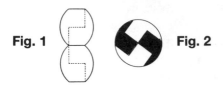

Fig. 1   Fig. 2

"Poem" Puzzle (page 92). The poem is about the letter "E."

"1995" Puzzle (page 93). There is sometimes more than one way to arrange the signs and digits to equal a specific value. We give you the ones that Mike came up with.

$$1)\ (1 \times (\sqrt{9} + \sqrt{9})) - 5\ = 1$$
$$2)\ (1 + 9) - (\sqrt{9} + 5)\ = 2$$
$$3)\ -1 + ((\sqrt{9 \times 9}) - 5) = 3$$
$$4)\ (-1 + 9) - (9 - 5)\ = 4$$
$$5)\ (1 + \sqrt{9 \times 9}) - 5\ = 5$$
$$6)\ 1 + (9 - 9) + 5\ = 6$$
$$7)\ ((1 \times 9) + \sqrt{9}) - 5\ = 7$$
$$8)\ 1 + 9 - (\sqrt{9 - 5})\ = 8$$
$$9)\ 1 + (9 \div \sqrt{9}) + 5\ = 9$$
$$10)\ -1 - \sqrt{9} + 9 + 5\ = 10$$

"Fours" Puzzle (page 94). Here's the solution Professor Flunkum finally came up with. Make-up class is Saturday, 7:00 a.m.

$$44 + \frac{44}{4} = 55$$

"Hippo" Puzzle (page 95). Take away the letter "S" from the word "SEVEN" and you're left with "EVEN." You've made seven even.

124

"Balloonist" Puzzle (page 96). This is a famous puzzle by the great Lewis Carroll. The first son, Rab, being a lawyer, worked at the *bar*, his name spelled backwards. Ymra's name certainly fit his profession, seeing that it was *Army* spelled backwards. So, the third son, who joined the Navy, should logically be named *Yvan*, a good Russian name.

In our second problem the plant in question is *Ivy*. It's pronounced I-V, which together is IV, the Roman numeral for 4.

"Store" Puzzle (page 97). Bascomb filled Fleurette's order by giving her five two-cent blue spools, fifty one-cent red spools, and eight five-cent green spools. This neatly came to $1.00, which made an easy transaction for Neville, the cashier.

"Automaton" Puzzle (page 98). The answer that Psycho came up with is 6,210,001,000. Note that the first digit, 6, is equal to the number of zeros in the number. The second digit, 2, is equal to the number of ones in the number. The third digit, 1, is equal to the number of twos in the number and so on.

"Subtraction" Puzzle (page 99). Alice found the solution when she passed through the looking glass. Once inside she looked back and found that the subtraction problem when reversed now read, "Nine minus one equals eight," which, of course, is correct. A tea party is called for after that one. (See drawing.)

"Balancing Card" Puzzle (page 100). When it's your turn to try the stunt you merely bend the card until it assumes a slight curve and then place it on the table. It will stand there for hours if left undisturbed. If the person you're betting with had tried to fold the card, explain to him that folding and creasing the card is not allowed. Chances are that he will not think of merely placing a slight bow in the card, and you, of course, will not mention to him that this is indeed permissible.

"Contest" Riddles (page 101). 1) A sponge; 2) in the Arkhives (archives); 3) the Mississippi River; 4) when he is out of patients (patience).

"Party" Puzzle (page 102). There were seven partygoers in the group and each item purchased cost $2.90. Seven times $2.90 comes to $20.30, the total amount of the purchases as given in the problem.

About the Author

Charles Barry Townsend has been writing books dealing with puzzles, games and magic for 26 years now. He is the author of 22 books, including *The World's Most Incredible Puzzles*, *The World's Hardest Puzzles*, *The World's Greatest Magic Tricks*, *Great Victorian Puzzle Book*, and *The World's Most Perplexing Puzzles*, all published by Sterling Publishing Company. Mr. Townsend lives in Mill Creek, Washington, where he spends a good deal of his time thinking up ways to confound and entertain readers like you.

Pictured below are the author and his dog, Jackie. They've just finished a new word puzzle featuring Jackie's favorite after-dinner treat. The puzzler has to change the word "milk" into the word "bone" in four moves. This puzzle is similar to the one presented on page 10. Jackie also wants to remind the reader not to miss the "Doggie" puzzle on page 57, which is presented by Jackie's friend Basil.

Answer: MILK, MILE, BILE, BOLE, BONE.

Index